PIANO . VOCAL . GUITAR

TOP DOWNLOADS 2009

ISBN 978-1-4234-8814-9

HAL•LEONARD®
CORPORATION

7777 W. BLUEMOUND RD. P.O. BOX 13819 MILWAUKEE, WI 53213

Visit Hal Leonard Online at
www.halleonard.com

BATTLEFIELD

Words and Music by LOUIS BIANCANIELLO,
WAYNE WILKINS, SAM WATTERS
and RYAN TEDDER

Slow groove

Don't try to ex-plain _ your mind; I know what's hap - 'nin' here.

One min-ute it's love, _ then sud-den-ly it's like a bat-tle-field.

One word turns in-to a war. Why is it the small-est things that tear _ us down? ____

BIG GREEN TRACTOR

Words and Music by JIM COLLINS
and DAVID LEE MURPHY

Moderately

She had a shin-y lit-tle Beem-er with the

rag top down, __ sit - tin' in the drive, but she would-n't get out. __ The

KNOCK YOU DOWN

Words and Music by KERI HILSON,
SHAFFER SMITH, KANYE WEST, NATE HILLS,
KEVIN COSSUM and MARCELLA ARAICA

Moderate R&B groove

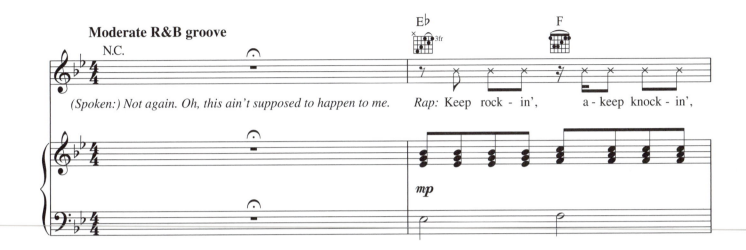

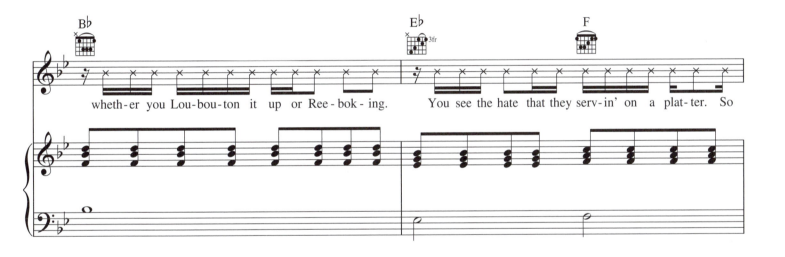

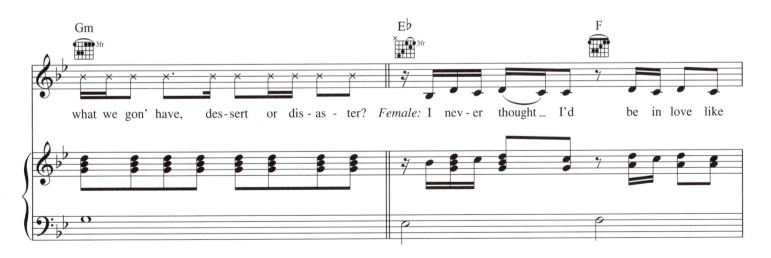

22

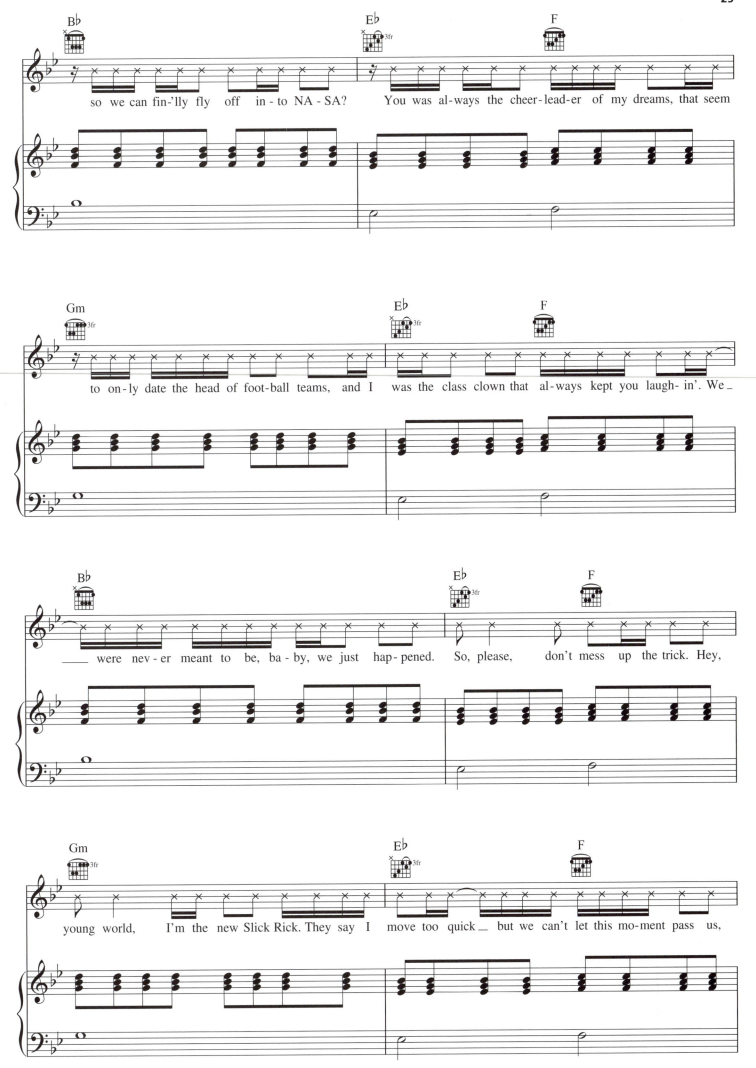

I GOTTA FEELING

Words and Music by WILL ADAMS,
ALLAN PINEDA, JAIME GOMEZ,
STACY FERGUSON, DAVID GUETTA
and FREDERIC RIESTERER

LOVE DRUNK

Words and Music by MARTIN JOHNSON,
DAVE KATZ and SAM HOLLANDER

LOVEGAME

Words and Music by STEFANI GERMANOTTA
and RedOne

Moderate Dance groove

Let's have some fun, this beat is sick. I wan-na take a ride on your dis-co stick. Let's

have some fun, this beat is sick. I wan-na take a ride on your dis-co stick.

Huh,   huh. ___

NEVER SAY NEVER

Words and Music by JOSEPH KING,
ISAAC SLADE and DAVID WELSH

ONE TIME

Words and Music by JAMES BUNTON,
CORRON TY KEE COLE, CHRISTOPHER STEWART
and THABISO NKHEREANYE

Moderately slow groove

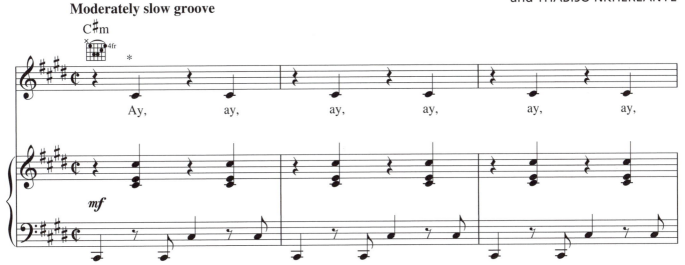

* Male vocal written at pitch.

yo.) _____ Your world _____ is my world, _____ and my fight _____

_____ is your fight, _____ and my breath _____ is your breath, _

_____ and your heart... _____ And now you're my one love, _ my

one heart, _ my one life _ for _ sure. Let me tell you one _

NEW DIVIDE

Words and Music by MIKE SHINODA,
JOE HAHN, BRAD DELSON,
ROB BOURDON, CHESTER BENNINGTON
and DAVE FARRELL

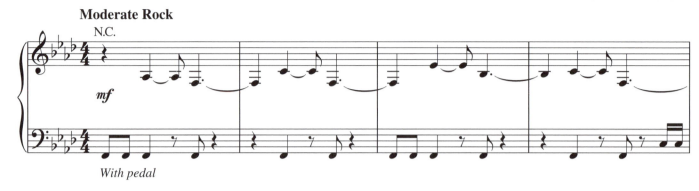

OBSESSED

Words and Music by MARIAH CAREY,
CHRISTOPHER STEWART and TERIUS NASH

Moderate groove

So, oh, ___ oh. ___ So, oh, ___ oh. So, oh, ___ oh. ___

So, oh, ___ oh. ___ So, oh, ___ oh. ___ So, oh, ___ oh. ___

So, oh, ___ oh. ___ So, oh. ___ All up in the blogs, ___

*Ad lib. on D.S.

PARTY IN THE U.S.A.

Words and Music by JESSICA CORNISH,
LUKASZ GOTTWALD and CLAUDE KELLY

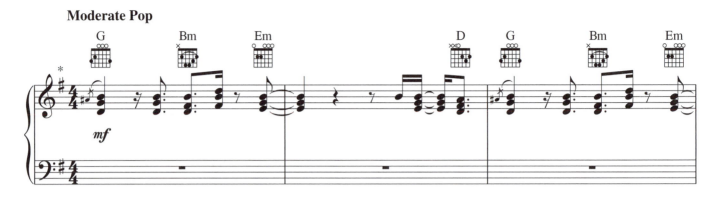

I hopped off the plane at L - A - X___ with a
Get to the club in my tax - i - cab.___ Ev - 'ry-

dream and my car - di - gan.___ Wel - come to the land of fame, ex - cess.___
bod - y's look - in' at me now, ___ like, "Who's that chick that's rock - in' kicks?___ She's

* *Recorded a half step lower.*

SHE WOLF

Words and Music by SHAKIRA,
JOHN HILL and SAM ENDICOTT

USE SOMEBODY

Words and Music by CALEB FOLLOWILL, NATHAN FOLLOWILL,
JARED FOLLOWILL and MATTHEW FOLLOWILL

Syncopated Rock

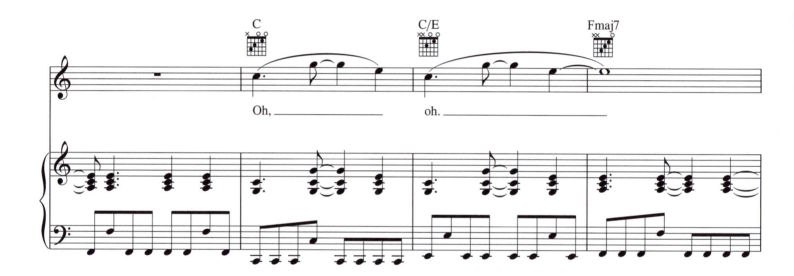

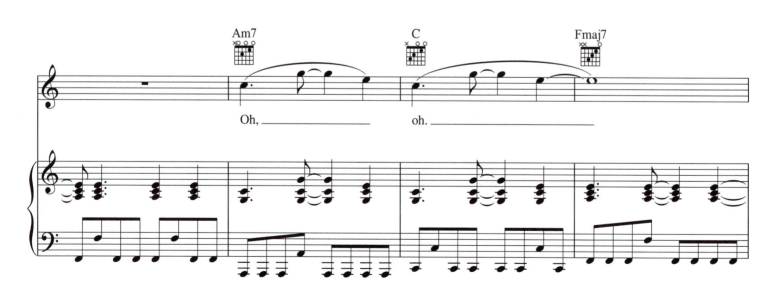

WAKING UP IN VEGAS

Words and Music by DESMOND CHILD,
KATY PERRY and ANDREAS CARLSSON

Upbeat Pop-Rock

You got-ta help me out; __

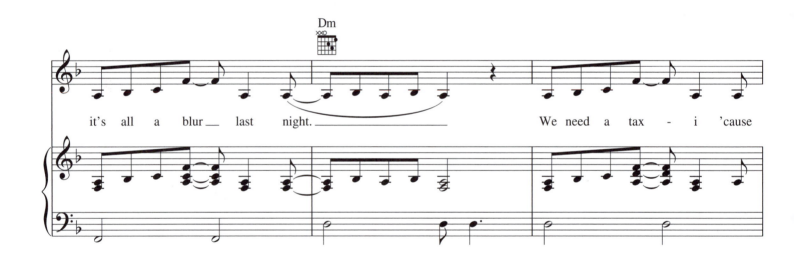

it's all a blur last night. _____ We need a tax-i 'cause

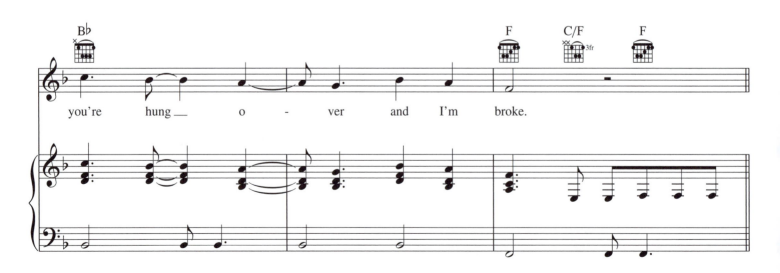

you're hung o-ver and I'm broke.

Re - mem - ber what you told me. _____ Re -

mem - ber what you told me, told _____ me, told me.

D.S. al Coda

Oh. _____

CODA

That's what you get, ba - by. Shake the glit -

YOU BELONG WITH ME

Words and Music by TAYLOR SWIFT
and LIZ ROSE

* Recorded a half step lower.

HAL•LEONARD ESSENTIAL SONGS

Play the best songs from the Roaring '20s to today! Each collection features dozens of the most memorable songs of each decade, or in your favorite musical style, arranged in piano/vocal/guitar format.

THE 1920s
Over 100 songs that shaped the decade: Ain't We Got Fun? • Basin Street Blues • Bye Bye Blackbird • Can't Help Lovin' Dat Man • I Wanna Be Loved by You • Makin' Whoopee • Ol' Man River • Puttin' On the Ritz • Toot, Toot, Tootsie • Yes Sir, That's My Baby • and more.
00311200 ....$24.95

THE 1930s
97 essential songs from the 1930s: April in Paris • Body and Soul • Cheek to Cheek • Falling in Love with Love • Georgia on My Mind • Heart and Soul • I'll Be Seeing You • The Lady Is a Tramp • Mood Indigo • My Funny Valentine • You Are My Sunshine • and more.
00311193 ....$24.95

THE 1940s
An amazing collection of over 100 songs from the '40s: Boogie Woogie Bugle Boy • Don't Get Around Much Anymore • Have I Told You Lately That I Love You • I'll Remember April • Route 66 • Sentimental Journey • Take the "A" Train • You'd Be So Nice to Come Home To • and more.
00311192 ....$24.95

THE 1950s
Over 100 pivotal songs from the 1950s, including: All Shook Up • Bye Bye Love • Chantilly Lace • Fever • Great Balls of Fire • Kansas City • Love and Marriage • Mister Sandman • Rock Around the Clock • Sixteen Tons • Tennessee Waltz • Wonderful! Wonderful! • and more.
00311191 ....$24.95

THE 1960s
104 '60s essentials, including: Baby Love • California Girls • Dancing in the Street • Hey Jude • I Heard It Through the Grapevine • Respect • Stand by Me • Twist and Shout • Will You Love Me Tomorrow • Yesterday • You Keep Me Hangin' On • and more.
00311190 ....$24.95

THE 1970s
Over 80 of the best songs from the '70s: American Pie • Band on the Run • Come Sail Away • Dust in the Wind • I Feel the Earth Move • Let It Be • Morning Has Broken • Smoke on the Water • Take a Chance on Me • The Way We Were • You're So Vain • and more.
00311189 ....$24.95

THE 1980s
Over 70 classics from the age of power pop and hair metal: Against All Odds • Call Me • Ebony and Ivory • The Heat Is On • Jump • Manic Monday • Sister Christian • Time After Time • Up Where We Belong • What's Love Got to Do with It • and more.
00311188 ....$24.95

Complete contents listings are available online at **www.halleonard.com**

THE 1990s
68 songs featuring country-crossover, swing revival, the birth of grunge, and more: Change the World • Fields of Gold • Ironic • Livin' La Vida Loca • More Than Words • Smells like Teen Spirit • Walking in Memphis • Zoot Suit Riot • and more.
00311187 ....$24.95

THE 2000s
59 of the best songs that brought in the new millennium: Accidentally in Love • Beautiful • Don't Know Why • Get the Party Started • Hey Ya! • I Hope You Dance • 1985 • This Love • A Thousand Miles • Wherever You Will Go • Who Let the Dogs Out • You Raise Me Up • and more.
00311186 ....$24.95

ACOUSTIC ROCK
Over 70 songs, including: About a Girl • Barely Breathing • Blowin' in the Wind • Fast Car • Landslide • Turn! Turn! Turn! (To Everything There Is a Season) • Walk on the Wild Side • and more.
00311747 ....$24.95

THE BEATLES
Over 90 of the finest from this extraordinary band: All My Loving • Back in the U.S.S.R. • Blackbird • Come Together • Get Back • Help! • Hey Jude • If I Fell • Let It Be • Michelle • Penny Lane • Something • Twist and Shout • Yesterday • more!
00311389 ....$24.95

BROADWAY
Over 90 songs of the stage: Any Dream Will Do • Blue Skies • Cabaret • Don't Cry for Me, Argentina • Edelweiss • Hello, Dolly! • I'll Be Seeing You • Memory • The Music of the Night • Oklahoma • Summer Nights • There's No Business Like Show Business • Tomorrow • more.
00311222 ....$24.95

CHILDREN'S SONGS
Over 110 songs, including: Bob the Builder "Intro Theme Song" • "C" Is for Cookie • Eensy Weensy Spider • I'm Popeye the Sailor Man • The Muppet Show Theme • Old MacDonald • Sesame Street Theme • and more.
00311823 ....$24.99

CHRISTMAS
Over 100 essential holiday favorites: Blue Christmas • The Christmas Song • Deck the Hall • Frosty the Snow Man • Joy to the World • Merry Christmas, Darling • Rudolph the Red-Nosed Reindeer • Silver Bells • and more!
00311241 ....$24.95

COUNTRY
96 essential country standards, including: Achy Breaky Heart • Crazy • The Devil Went down to Georgia • Elvira • Friends in Low Places • God Bless the U.S.A. • Here You Come Again • Lucille • Redneck Woman • Tennessee Waltz • and more.
00311296 ....$24.95

JAZZ STANDARDS
99 jazz classics no music library should be without: Autumn in New York • Body and Soul • Don't Get Around Much Anymore • Easy to Love (You'd Be So Easy to Love) • I've Got You Under My Skin • The Lady Is a Tramp • Mona Lisa • Satin Doll • Stardust • Witchcraft • and more.
00311226 ....$24.95

LOVE SONGS
Over 80 romantic hits: Can You Feel the Love Tonight • Endless Love • From This Moment On • Have I Told You Lately • I Just Called to Say I Love You • Love Will Keep Us Together • My Heart Will Go On • Wonderful Tonight • You Are So Beautiful • more.
00311235 ....$24.95

LOVE STANDARDS
100 romantic standards: Dream a Little Dream of Me • The Glory of Love • I Left My Heart in San Francisco • I've Got My Love to Keep Me Warm • The Look of Love • A Time for Us • You Are the Sunshine of My Life • and more.
00311256 ....$24.95

MOVIE SONGS
94 of the most popular silver screen songs: Alfie • Beauty and the Beast • Chariots of Fire • Footloose • I Will Remember You • Jailhouse Rock • Moon River • People • Somewhere Out There • Summer Nights • Unchained Melody • and more.
00311236 ....$24.95

ROCK
Over 80 essential rock classics: Black Magic Woman • Day Tripper • Free Bird • A Groovy Kind of Love • I Shot the Sheriff • The Joker • My Sharona • Oh, Pretty Woman • Proud Mary • Rocket Man • Roxanne • Takin' Care of Business • A Whiter Shade of Pale • Wild Thing • more!
00311390 ....$24.95

TV SONGS
Over 100 terrific tube tunes, including: The Addams Family Theme • Bonanza • The Brady Bunch • Desperate Housewives Main Title • I Love Lucy • Law and Order • Linus and Lucy • Sesame Street Theme • Theme from the Simpsons • Theme from the X-Files • and more!
00311223 ....$24.95

WEDDING
83 songs of love and devotion: All I Ask of You • Canon in D • Don't Know Much • Here, There and Everywhere • Love Me Tender • My Heart Will Go On • Somewhere Out There • Wedding March • You Raise Me Up • and more.
00311309 ....$24.95

FOR MORE INFORMATION, SEE YOUR LOCAL MUSIC DEALER, OR WRITE TO:

HAL•LEONARD®
CORPORATION
7777 W. BLUEMOUND RD. P.O. BOX 13819 MILWAUKEE, WI 53213

Prices, contents and availability subject to change without notice.

0209